STRENGTH OF THE SMALL

A Collection of Poems

Joan AMBU

ISBN: 0-9836996-3-1
ISBN-13: 978-0-9836996-3-7

Library of Congress Control Number: 2012914322

Printed in the United States of America by CreateSpace
North Charleston, South Carolina

Acknowledgement

To Jesus Christ, my Lord and Savior
Mold me, shape me and feed me Lord. With your knowledge, that I may absorb and retain; that I may learn and gain.

Eduardo, my husband
Thank you for your understanding, patience, support, availability, encouragement, praises and unconditional love. Thank you for entertaining our children while I spent countless hours putting this book together.

Ivan and Naomi, my children
Thank you for being my inspiration. Thank you for your constant cheers and patience. I love you.

Mary Asakwa and Pauline Azah, my aunts
Though I didn't get to see you often growing up, I felt so loved and appreciated around you. You both showed me that quality surpasses quantity by your actions and deeds.

Jose Perez, my father-in-law
From the moment I met you, you have always made me feel welcomed in your home. You shower your grandchildren with love and gifts. For these little gestures that mean so much to me; I thank you, Dad, from the bottom of my heart.

My family and friends
Thank you for your love, moral support and for the breaks needed to work on my books.

Stéphane Tchoudja Nana
My childhood friend, my best friend and confidant; whose presence had a grounding effect and still does.
Thank you for all that you have done for me.

My readers
Thank you so much for your faithfulness, for the feedbacks and the wonderful words of encouragement that I continuously receive from you.
I am humbled over your appreciation for what I do.

Thank you all for standing tough and pulling through with me. Your faithfulness will always be remembered!

Foreword

"I am a conscious being in a constant state of gratitude." As Joan Ambu simply puts it, when referring to her relationship with others. Accepting, forgiving and loving others is exactly what she describes in Strength of The Small, her fourth book of poetry, which covers topics such as death, love, forgiveness, hope, innocence, gratitude and her quest for the knowledge of the Word.

The author is one who grew up and went to school right in my hands. A natural born poet who could compose and sing short verse songs. She grew up to be very fond of nature. She was always in the company of her class mates who loved and admired her talent.

I love to read her short stories, which she would come in and say "uncle, I have something new for you." I do not have a favorite poem as each single one is as powerful as the next. Every one of us can relate to a story as they are all about life experiences and lessons. Her poems are beautiful, powerful and healing.

Strength of the Small is about finding contentment and being at peace in every given situation.

George Usongo
School teacher and leader of the people.

Contents

Acknowledgement i
Foreword iii

Thought on Love. 13

Pretty Amélie 15
Unknown 16
To Be Near You 17
Without A Flow 18
Will I Ever Forgive You? 19
Wrong Turn 20
Growing Pain 21
Praying For You 22
Words Left Unspoken 23
Mothers' Daughter 24
Guilty Conscience 25

Thought on Kindness. 27

Loveless 29
Remember — 30
Dear Friend 31
A True Mother 32
Mold Me Lord 34
"In My Shoes" 36
Gratitude 39

Boundaries 40

Should Have 42
Strength of The Small 43
Choices 44
Love Is True 46
Pain of Death 47

Thought on Belief. 49

I Do Love You 51
Home 53
Loving You Still 54
Innocence 55
Pray for Me, Mama 57
Ungrateful 59
Let Me Go 61

Thought on Care. 63

I've Learned 65
I Do Not Wish For a Funeral 68
Wholeness 70
Restore My Peace 71

Thought on Embrace. 73

A Good Day to Die 75
Live The Moment 79
Release Me 81
Joy 82
Memory 83
You Were Always With Me 85
Be Gone, Fear! 86

You Ended Our Lives 87

Last Word/Last Man Standing   89
My Father Loves Me   90

Thought on Tolerance.   *91*

A Childhood Friendship   93
Remember —   95

About the Author   97
By the same Author   99

Thought on Love.

"If Kindness could be passed along, unrestrainedly, as forward messages, the World would be a better place."
– Joan AMBU

Pretty Amélie

She's the beautiful girl next door
Who's never ask for more.

Her name is Amélie
She's really pretty
And she's a nerd.
Third born of her family
Her heart is full of empathy
When one needs to be heard.

Shy girl with brown eyes
She proudly carries her head on her shoulders
With a genuine smile that never lies
When she's amongst others.

Beloved Amélie
As I often write in my diary
Is kind, wise and friendly
Simple and yet sophisticated
She doesn't need the magic of a fairy
To make her life uncomplicated.

I Love Amélie
As I love the scent of a Lily
Freshly picked in the morning.
She's my friend
My reason to stop mourning
My confident till the end.

Unknown

Even now I can feel it
Buried somewhere deep inside
Watching me
Wanting me
Waiting for me.

But do you know what scares me the most?
When I can't fight it anymore
When the sorrow takes over
When I totally lose control
When my strength gives up on me.

To Be Near You

My entire life is a prayer
In this soul of mine.
My life has just one desire
Where hope, peace and love combine
To give life to happiness:
My dream is to be near you.

They say I have to change
They call me "old game"
They say I am mysterious
And whatever else
But if they can't understand me
How can they reach me?

They don't know who I am
They don't know what I want
And they may never know
Because what I want dear Lord: is to be near you.

Without A Flow

The day is slow
Without a flow
The day is slow
And took on a warm glow
This I know for sure.

Time goes by
While reading a brochure
Sitting on a rock below
On a lazy day by the shore
Without a flow
I can't deny.
This I know for sure.

Will I Ever Forgive You?

Who could imagine such a thing of you?
Who could think you would turn away from me?
Who could imagine you would treat me this way?
I thought you truly cared
I thought I was a part of you
But today, I am ashamed of you.

Will I ever forgive you?
Will this pain forever remain?
Will I forgive you one day
As you took my joy away?

Sometimes, I don't believe I know you.
Still I hope
Still I pray
That before my dying hour
I will know the peace that comes from forgiveness
I will experience the joy that comes from letting go.

Wrong Turn

As a child I was perfect
Not exactly perfect because no one is.
But as a child I knew what I wanted
Back then I knew right from wrong
I knew my limits and my boundaries
I knew I wanted to grow-up
Grow-up and be independent.
I wanted to achieve self-love
I wanted to be complete and happy.

As I matured and became a Woman
It seemed I forgot all about my values
It seemed I got so desperate
That I forgot to put myself first.
I got carried away
Loosing myself in the process
And realized I made a wrong turn.

Fortunately I've lived long enough
To know there is a light shining at the end of the tunnel.
My Son opened a new door for me
He gave me hope for a new beginning:
That I can do it on my own
Because I'm stronger and wiser now
Because it's time I made a right turn
Because it's never too late
And because I deserve to be happy.

Growing Pain

I have become a shell once again
All I do is give, no gain.
I never knew giving could hurt this much
I never knew I could hurt this much.

I love a man who doesn't see it
I need a man who doesn't need me.
What I do doesn't matter, I know it
He's simply fallen out of love with me.

I ache to feel you
One more time, to please you.
You reject me, it's not right
I'm in pain, I'm not alright.

How can I live pass this?
I'm so broken inside.
How can you treat me this way?
I'm torn inside.
What did I do to deserve this?
Perhaps I should stay away.

Praying For You

Here we are again
Wanting someone to explain
To ease the pain
Yet it remains…

Death takes no side
Where pain resides
Death takes no pride
When someone dies.

Far from controversy
Death has no mercy
Forced to say goodbye
The hurts multiply.

Though we so painfully decry
God hears our cry.

Words Left Unspoken

Dear God
For so long
I couldn't understand
All the sorrow around me.
When I looked deep down
And saw the truth
I resented it
Yet, I protected it.
And for so long
I let it live free.

Today in my despair
While praying for enlightenment
You met me right where I was.
My heart is finally at peace
The weight has been lifted
The shame is gone forever.
My Lord Almighty
Now I clearly see
Why you placed me
Into this broken family of Men.

I renounce evil
I shall not be part of injustice
I shall not be divided
I shall not be moved
I shall not be corrupted.
I embrace my fate
For it is the task you appointed to me.

Mothers' Daughter

I am my Mothers' Daughter
Born before the sun rose up
Perhaps born too late.
Feelings all mixed-up
Today I learned my fate
I've lost my laughter.

I am my own reflection
My soul is consumed by affliction
My heart for a while was corrupt
I was blinded by the lie.
The night was too abrupt
I didn't hear you cry.

I can't have another
I've lost my Mother.

Guilty Conscience

So, it has begun
Your conscience demands justice
You are stunned
Wish you were a Praying Mantis
A little more mindful
Less neglectful.

You've made a choice
A foolish decision
For which you are now paying the price
Mind and Soul in Chaotic fusion.
Didn't have to be this way, you know
No, oh no.

At the end of the day
It's just you and your demons
Even an opened window
Can't save you from what has been foreshadowed
Come on, come on
I told you so one day.

Suddenly I'm the woe
Yet you look for me at every corner.
To completely eradicate me
You must first find me
Your quest is a drainer
Tell me, who's the foe?

Have you lately
Done something premeditatedly?
When you faced your reflection
Were you overawed?
Did you like what you saw?
Are you ready to change direction?
To mend this relation?
Or suffer more rejection?

The name of God is hallowed
He is your owner
Seek Him rather sooner
You can't hide from your shadow.
He can put an end to this hell
Through Him your blessings dwell.

Thought on Kindness.

"Kindness is the catalyst that fuels our drive for love and compassion." – Joan AMBU

Loveless

I do not hate you
Hate is powerless
Hate is my inability to communicate
Hate is how I feel inside.

I do not hate you
Hate is faceless
Hate is a treacherous silhouette
Disguising as a friend when my guards are down.

I do not hate you
It's just so hard to admit
That I'm the one who needs to change
That I need to heal on my own
That I need to put my pieces back together
That I have to become whole again
And be grateful for BEING.

I do not hate you
Hate is judgmental
It robs me of an opportunity to know you
It robs me of an opportunity to be known
It ties me down
And I'm not free.

I must not hate you.

Remember —

"Hate is nothing but a feeling that consumes us all
in a moment of despair and sorrow;
a moment of regret and envy." – Joan AMBU

We must not hate.

Dear Friend

Love, Life
Different world
Different dreams
Wish, Hope
A better day
A better way
Sing, Shout
My heart awaits
Open wide
Dance, Rejoice
You are so far away
My dear friend

Love, love more
I wish my words
Bring you great comfort

A True Mother

Child of mine
Innocent and dear
You are my pride
I am your caregiver
I am your guide
I love you forever.

I was a single woman visiting a friend
In the same hospital where you were born in
There I was, in my late 30s, single
Unsure of what my future held for me
Yet, happy to be.

As I walked through the maternity ward
I saw you for the first time
My heart melted at your sight
I believed strongly
That you would be mine
I care lovingly
When the nurse placed you in my arms.

I didn't get to love you from the start
I didn't birth you
And while you were laying
Confused and scared
Anxiously waiting
For your mama who never came...
I noticed you
You were perfect
I chose.

I chose you
Child of mine
Beautiful and helpless
I chose you
To love and nurture
To protect and respect
To educate and set free.

When you're ready
And that day comes
To start your own family
Don't be afraid and trust yourself
That in the midst of everything
You can make it on your own
Remember, Child
Once all is said and done
We all belong to the World.

You are my Child
I am your Mother
I loved you then
I love you with everything I am.

Mold Me Lord

My Lord and Redeemer
I am a Child with no direction
As I call upon your name
To guide me through the right path
I ask that you show me
Your merciful ways.

My Lord and Savior
I am a Woman with many flaws
I kneel before you today
Praying and asking
That you give me the ability
To love unconditionally as you do.

You are my Master
You are my King
I am your servant
I am at your mercy.

Mold me Lord
Shape me
Feed me Lord
With your knowledge
That I may absorb and retain
That I may learn and gain.

I am a dried up tree
Revive me
I am a damaged picture
Convert my million pieces into your patchwork
Show me the light
Relight my fire
Scar me with your Word
So when my time comes to pass
I may burst into infinite little pieces
Infecting mankind with your Unfathomable Love.

"In My Shoes"

I died the other night
Alone and scared of the unknown
Yet, happy to meet my Father
I died on my own terms.

If you knew me and mourn
I want you to know
That I thought of you
I prayed for you
That you may find closure
I prayed for myself
And found my answer.

I died the other night
I made a choice
I chose what was best for me
I wasn't weak
I had made up my mind
I wasn't a coward
It took all of my strength
To do what I had to.

You're blaming me
Without knowing me
You're condemning me
Before hearing me
You're making your own assumptions
Based on your personal fears
Do not speculate
Pray for your own soul.

I should have sought a different path
You now say
I should have turned to God
You now say
But I tell you
Fighting the good fight
Is not as easy
When you're fighting alone.

I didn't lose the battle
I'm right where I wanted to be.
I am home
Happy with my Father.

Yes, I died the other night
You may have known of me or not
And while I needed all the help I could get
You were too busy with life
To hear my cry for help
You didn't care much then.
Do not judge me now
You weren't there for me.

I have no regrets
I have found my higher ground
You didn't let me down
It was meant to be
In losing you
I found myself.

Love one another
Be there for each other
Do not wait until the end
To feel guilty or condemn
Do not judge me now
You weren't there for me.

Gratitude

Good morning World
What a beautiful day
What a precious gift
I have been given today.
Spirit uplift
Joy to bequeath
To awake and breathe
To put on my shoes and twirl.

Thank you, Jesus
For caring for us.
Today is a good day
I'm grateful to be alive
I'm grateful to live this life
To embrace whatever comes my way.

Your words are reviving and precise
I belong to a family of great Men
And this alone should suffice
Amen, Amen, Amen!

Boundaries

I am an entity
My flaws are not silenced
I give them words
They give me strength
My joy is contagious
My love can mend a broken heart.

I am a believer
A fervent servant of my Lord
A woman of few words
Eager to share my Faith with you
As I explore this mysterious World
Created for you and me.

We are One
One distinct species
Sharing so many features
Yet, different in so many ways
Fighting for the last word
Fighting for recognition.

You are a blessing in your own way
Your presence is cherished
Your opinion counts as much as mine
Your Faith is as important to you as mine is to me
I know
I will not intrude
But hope
We can teach each other how to grow love.

I am a piece of History
As I touch your life
Scaring you with selfless love
That never complains
And never demands in return
I can only hope
That my Life, in the end
Will be remembered.

Should Have

Should have
It's easier said than done
Could you really have kept your promise?

Should have
It's ok, you know
It's done, big deal!
There's no need for regrets
You can't turn back time.
I know
Yes I know
You wished you had
A second chance
But you know quite well
That back then
You wouldn't have
Done it differently.

Strength of The Small

My heart, my mind
Your sight, your pride
I'm just a child
You are the adult
Excuse me, I hope you don't mind
I have been called 'naive'
And of course you are 'the brain'
It all makes sense
Until we are put to the test.

Don't look down on me
Unless you need my help
Don't talk about me
Unless you are praising me.

In the end
We are pretty much the same
I may be small
But my Faith is strong
Now you know
It's the Strength of The Small.

Choices

Childless Woman
By choice or medical reason
You are my daughter, sister, aunt
I love, value and honor you
Your contribution to society is appreciated
You are a beautiful person.

I choose Motherhood
And all the responsibility
Because I have so much to give
I have so much to share and pass on
Whatever your reasons for childlessness are
They are yours and I respect them.

Your choice of childlessness
Doesn't make you selfish.
My choice of Motherhood
Doesn't make me 'old'
Given we're not walking in each other's shoes
We should eliminate assumptions.

We both value our independence
Let's not look at each other differently
We used to have good moments
I still cherish every single one of them
Nothing has changed
We've simply chosen different paths.

Children are a gift from God
Nothing compares to the joy of loving
Nothing should impair your quest for freedom.
As much as couples must learn to compromise in
marriage
Childless couples and parents alike
Must find a way to maintain a sane relation.

Love Is True

Love Simply
Be there Faithfully
Educate Lovingly
Communicate Openly
Await Patiently
Forgive Truly
Live Fully.

When you give of yourself
Give what you can freely.
And when you love
Love completely
Because real love is true.

Pain of Death

Death, you must know
Is a loner
Is not sociable
It doesn't negotiate
It doesn't give a second chance
It doesn't sympathize.

To some it can be gentle
And to others, unkind
Either way
The outcome is the same
When a loved one cease
The living is thorn.

Pray and be prayerful
Do not find joy in another's grief
Do not let your anger destroy your dreams
Look around you
Be grateful for what you have
Keep your faith alive and your heart open.

Regardless of circumstances
Death is nothing to rejoice about
As much as it comes as a relief to some
It leaves others empty
And robs them of an opportunity
To cherish the ones who have ceased.

Thought on Belief.

"Claim your loved ones in Jesus name so that their path will be true and safe." – Joan AMBU

I Do Love You

I love you
Believe me, I really do.
I've said and done things
I wish I could take back
I haven't been at my best for a while
I haven't kept all my promises.

Every now and then
I keep reverting to what I know
I'm not proud of myself
I'm not done fighting the good fight
I love you
Believe me, I really do.

I've been miserable living without you
Nothing's the same since you left
I don't know how much longer
I can keep this masquerade
I'm starting to break down
Falling into pieces.

Slowly but surely
I'm rapidly running out of options
For the first time I'm afraid
I hope you understand
I love you
Believe me, I really do.

I understand why you've fallen out of love
I wasn't the best I could be
I didn't invest enough into us
There's a chance, I'm sure
That I destroyed your dreams
Along with mine.

As a person of many flaws
I can only thank you
For standing tough with me
Forgive me
I love you
Believe me, I really do.

It's probably over
I'm hurt but not surprised
In my heart I know I've lost you
I had you and I foolishly let you go
I love you
Believe me, I really do.

I may never find love again
I can no longer be a prisoner of love
Set me free
That I may use the time
To gather what's left
Of any chance to happiness.

I love you
Believe me, I really do.

Home

My Small Home
My beautiful Strong Home!
How I love being here
Wrapped in the safety of your walls
How good it feels to hear
Our neighbors complimenting.

I am glad I chose you
The smallest and weakest of them all
There you were
Standing Strong
Waiting for me to unveil
The beauty within the walls.

Your barren land which bared no fruit
Has now turned into an enchanted garden
The Earth so dry
That weed would fight to stay alive
Is now alive with colors
So lovely and bright.

I do not know
I do not linger
I found you
I feel happy within you
You've given me more than I need
And your beauty grows like a wild weed.

Loving You Still

My heart's been broken
So many times
So often my kindness has been taken for granted
Used by people I never expected
Barely loved
Loved for the wrong reasons.

My heart's been broken
Stolen, abused, betrayed
I wish I had a safe place
A little piece of Heaven
I could call my own
To find myself and heal.

Days like this I feel empty
Used, bitter, resentful
I no longer see the person I love
I see a reason to get away from it all
To bury all the memories
And take a deep breath of Hope.

I am grateful however
That in the midst of it all
My heart can mend itself
When it's surrounded by love
And once all has been said and done
I'm loving you still.

Innocence

I was born free
Without personal sin...

Teach me acceptance
Teach me tolerance
Talk to me about your experience
Share your grievance
Share your strife
Warn me about the danger of Life.

Do not fill my mind with hate
Teach me to appreciate
Do not rob me of my innocence
Allow me to see the World's magnificence
To bear my own consequence
To witness mankind's ignorance
To experience indifference
To practice vigilance
To feel Love
To share Love
Knowledge does not update itself
Allow me to think for myself.

Do not add a twist to my fate
Hatred is not innate
Do not take away my joy
Do not shape me to destroy
Whenever you are upset
Remember, time we cannot reset.

Believe me
I will not forget
Do not scar me
I will regret.

Pray for Me, Mama

Mama
Oh, dear Mama
I am in so much pain
The World is spinning around me
My heart aches
I can't see clearly.
I am in so much pain
Pray for me, Mama.

I have thought of you today
More than any other day
I have called you randomly
Just to hear your voice
And ask about my Brothers.
I told you about my dream:
That my Sister met my Children
And I had never seen her as happy.
She smiled at me, Mama
I smiled back.

Mama
Oh, dear Mama
I am in so much pain
I wish I could call you
To tell you about my hurts.

I wish I could hear your voice, Mama
To ask you to pray for me, Mama
But I know what it would do to you
It would tear you apart
To hear me cry this much
And I could never forgive myself
For stripping you of your joy of New Year's Eve,
tonight.

I hope the magical bond we shared for 9 months
Has not been totally broken
That somehow you can feel my pain
And pray for me.
Pray that I may regain my strength
To smile again
To Love again
To do the things I like to do
To serve my Lord fervently
To hear your voice again.

Mama,
Oh, dear Mama
Pray for me tonight.

Ungrateful

I loved you when no one would
I loved you when no one could

There was a time when you were in need
A time when Life seemed so unfair to you
When the Earth stood still
And your candle light went out.

You came to me a few times
For financial help
For advice and moral support
And I provided for you
Without second-guessing myself
Without regrets.

I believed you were truthful about your needs
I believed you desperately needed a helping hand
Maybe I was just a mean to an end
Maybe you thought I never understood the rules of the
game
And thought I was an easy target
I will never know for sure.

Why are you so ungrateful?
Why do you complain about me?
I was there for you
When no one would
When no one could
I was there to comfort you
To lend an ear and to cheer you up.

I pray for you
I do not regret helping you
And if I had to do it all over
I would.

Let Me Go

We were young when we met
Young and full of Life
We were excited about Life
Excited about our Life together
We had expectations and dreams
We dreamt of a pain-free World.

We were happy
We pursue our dreams
We contributed to society
We started a Family
I changed
I grew up
You did not
You remained a child at mind.

I loved you
And I love you still.
Our priorities have changed
We have lost our vision
I am losing my individuality
My feelings are numb.

Set me free
I am ready to move on
My fate is not linked to yours
My happiness is not determined by my past
I can make it on my own
Let me go.

Thought on Care.

"Each time we hurt someone; we lose a piece of ourselves."
– Joan AMBU

I've Learned

I've learned
That knowledge does not update itself
And even though I'm constantly learning
I must keep my mind active.

I've learned
That I must save life
Even if at some point in time
That life will end mine.

I've learned
That hate, though not contagious
Is a self-destructive illness
And I must not practice it.

I've learned
That Blessings come in small packages
I must not hold on to perishable things
When all I really need is around me.

I've learned
That appearance can be deceiving
We judge people by the image they portray to the
World
Rather than the person within.

I've learned
That you cannot envy someone
Until you walk in their shoes
And embrace their flaws.

I've learned
That the pain of death
Has the power to bring people together
And end feuds.

I've learned
That if I do not have something constructive to say
About someone or something
I must keep my mouth shut
And hope that when my actions come to light
Mankind will be merciful.

I've learned
That a simple "I Love You"
Goes a long way
It heals the most incurable disease.

I've learned
That when we have a heated argument
And you hurt my feelings
That's precisely when I must not betray your trust.

I've learned
That I must always be true to myself
No matter what others think
That I must be grateful at all times
Because Life can end abruptly.

I've learned
That when I feel lonely
And the World seems to ignore my cry for help
I must keep trusting
In the One who watches over me and never sleeps
I must be patient and keep trusting
Because He has never let me down.

I Do Not Wish For a Funeral

I am still here
I have not changed
Nothing has changed
I breathe, I see, I hear, I feel
Talk to me
Stand by me faithfully
Love me truly
Celebrate my life every day.

Rejoice with me always
Laugh and make me laugh
Make beautiful memories
Do not regret
Do not hold back feelings from me
Celebrate my life now
You cannot make up
For anything once I am gone.

I do not wish for a funeral.

Why are you here?
How did you get here so fast?
You barely acknowledged me
I left your World
You must have heard
But why are you here?
Why now?
Why is it so important to you?

You never cared
You never pretended to care
Now I am gone
Gone, to never return
Gone to a place free of pain
Why did you come here?
To see for yourself?
For a last good-bye?
You are too late...

I do not wish for a funeral.

Wholeness

What am I to you?
A person you can use
When you're in need?
A thing you can misuse
When you desire?
An object you can release your anger on
When things go astray?
Your World
When the skies are blue?

You do not own me
I am not an object
I am not a thing
I am one Soul
I am one body
I am a work in progress.

You cannot keep me down
You cannot break my Spirit
You cannot take away my dignity
I am whole.

Restore My Peace

Thank you God
For all the blessings in my life
For my beautiful Family and Friends
Who keep me grounded
When the World seems to fall apart
Thank you.

I need you so much
I am at a cross road
Give me a sign
Show me which way to go
I know you hear my cry
I know you are always with me.

You created me for a purpose
To live on this Earth
To live and serve you
Sometimes it's hard to see
What's in front of me
When I am broken inside.

Whenever I am lonely and lost
Make your face shine upon me
Whenever I am in doubt
Let the breeze gently caress my face
Let the wind carry my troubles away
And restore my peace

Show me which way to go.

Thought on Embrace.

"When it comes to Love; live the moment. It will make all the difference." – Joan AMBU

A Good Day to Die

It's a beautiful day
Breeze gently blowing through my hair
The sun shines so bright
The birds singing in harmony
All gathered at my window
I feel light
I have gained new strengths
The night took my pain away.

I am standing at a crossroad
Happy to have made it here
Happy to know that the choice has been made for me.
This day of awareness
Has led me down the road of certainty
A path of clarity.

My children came from all corners of the Earth
They came with their children
And their children brought their own children
For a last good-bye
For an opportunity to share
For a chance to create our last memories
I am in awe of my family
My Lord has been faithful to His words.

Spirit lifted up
Hands raised up in praise
Heart overwhelmed by the intensity of the moment
Tears of joy rolling down my face
Vibrant energy filling the air

I watched as they celebrated my life.
Memories flashed through my mind
Everything froze around me
Time suddenly stopped
With my Creator's consent
The Universe conspired in my favor
To heal my ache and set me free
To be reborn, at last
To be reborn into a new life.

What a good day to die.

Love that Strengthens:
Thoughts for My Father

I love my father; I really do.

He is one of the sweetest men I know
Not the easiest person to live with
But a good Man
A Man of honorable character
Who has had his share of experiences.
I often allow my heart to melt and speak to him
And once in a while I celebrate his life
I learned to act swiftly when it comes to a loved one.

My father is my biggest fan
He is proud of me
He rejoices over me
He's loved and nurtured me for as long as I can
remember
And he does it still.
He was my mentor, my best friend
Before I could understand
And appreciate the meaning of friendship.

While the Earth stopped moving around us
And the Lord revealed His plans for us
We experienced the love of God
that strengthens and renews
We experienced the love of God
that comforts and assures.

For the first eighteen years of my life
I learned tremendously from him.
Some people judged him by what they saw him to be
And others by what they knew him to be.
Yes, my father was a disciplinarian
However, those he thought
Knew they would be going to bigger,
better things in their life
Those who knew him or got to know him well
regarded him with respect.

I am my father's daughter
I have learned so much about the gift of giving by
watching him.
We give of ourselves totally
We give of our time freely to those in need.

Live The Moment

Life is unpredictable
Emotions are controllable
Hurts can be curable
Mistakes can be correctable
Lies can be concealable
Once discovered condemnable
Words can be damageable
Stay true and humble.

A good heart is desirable
Laughter is enjoyable
Love you should enable
When true, it's insatiable
Bitterness you must disable
Hatred is unjustifiable
Fame is just a label
You are more than able.

Dreams are achievable
Success is attainable
Honor is commendable
Failure is not acceptable
For every action you enable
You will be accountable
God's love is unfathomable
His faithfulness immeasurable.

Material is perishable
A loved one is irreplaceable
A broken heart can be irreparable
A bad memory unforgettable
Time wasted is irretrievable
Good deeds are redeemable.

Live the moment
Cherish the moment.

Release Me

Release me from this chain
That is wrapped around my heart
Release me from this pain
That is weighing down my mind
Release me from this sorrow
Stop my bleeding with the yarrow
Keep me on the chart
Allow my soul to bind.

Release my mind
Release my soul
Release my very being.

I feel my body strain
Allow my emotions to drain
Bring down the rain
To wash away my stain
Don't let me suffer in vain
Keep me sane
Drop me off this train
That has trapped me in my brain.

Make the pain go
Let the sorrow flee
So that maybe, just maybe
I can someday feel free.

Joy

Joy, oh joy!
We all need it
It's impossible to live without it
Seek it
Once found
Strive to keep it.

Memory

'Hold me, I am scared,'
I would ask of you each night
At the end of the scary bed time stories
Our older cousin chose to tell.
Each night, you held me tight
'Don't worry, they are just stories
I am here, she declared'
In her arms, asleep I fell.

She was truly one of a kind
One great example to mankind
She turned out to be one phenomenal Woman
One faithful Woman
Who always fought the good fight
Whose future seemed bright.

At the end of each day
It was never my way or her way
It was all about us
As we sang in chorus.
Our paths always aligned
We remembered that we only had each other
All we had was each other
I had her back and she had mine.

From the moment I became aware
I claimed her
My sister, my friend, blood of my blood.
I truly cared
I claimed her

And God made her mine.

Now a simple object can take me back
To that point when I last saw her face.

You Were Always With Me

I came from the West
Ready and determined
To meet the One who never sleeps.
Passing through the North
Traveling as each day brought me closer to you
Sustained by faith
Eager to find you
The One who renews.

I heard so much about you
I learned nothing thrives without you
I witnessed people swear by you
I saw lives changed through you
I too, became amazed by you
And I am now walking to meet you.

The rain always left traces for me to follow
The wind brought hints of your soul to my doorsteps
Nature whispered your name
Which echoed through my heart
The Clouds formed shapes
Directing me to the right path.

I came from the West
Willing and determined
Eager to find you.
I arrived at my destination
To realized
That you were always with me.

Be Gone, Fear!

I am free again
Free to express myself
Free to control my feelings
Free to live the life I was meant to live.

I dreamt of this day
Without knowing when it would come
I dreamt of the things I would say to you
When at last, I had the courage.

I let you live under my skin for so long
That I am unsure I can make it without you
You corrupted my mind
You suppressed my senses.

By coming face to face with you
I found the strength to eradicate you
I found peace that comes with acceptance
I found hope.

Be gone, fear!
And let me be the Woman I was meant to be.

You Ended Our Lives

This day wasn't meant for us
At least, we didn't think so
This hate crime shouldn't have happened
We didn't do anything wrong
You didn't even know us
Why did you take us away from our loved ones?

You ended our lives.

Our day had just begun
We all gathered for a meal
We didn't expect it to happen in a temple
Your intrusion took us by surprise
We were not ready to go
You didn't give us a chance.

You ended our lives.

For a while we were forced to watch our backs
We were threatened
We were victimized and terrorized
We lived in constant fear
Yet, we hoped still
For a change of some sort.

You ended our lives.

We had lives of our own
We were alive and happy
We had duties and responsibilities
We had families and friends
We had dreams too, you know
Which are now just memories.

You ended our lives.

We knew a day would come
A day chosen for us by our Creator
We didn't expect it to happen today
We didn't expect it to happen here
We didn't expect it to be tragic
We didn't expect it to end by your hand.

You ended our lives.

Last Word/Last Man Standing

You didn't win an argument
Because you had the last word
You are your words
You won because you made them real
In a way only you possibly could
You lost because they hurt
And you can't take them back
You gave them life.

You think you won the fight
Because you are the last man standing
You think it's over
Because you subdued your opponent
You think you're untouchable
Because no one dares to fight you.

Don't be too quick at celebrating
You should remember there's an old saying,
'Every dog has its day'
And mine is just waiting.

My Father Loves Me

I am a Child of God
My Father loves me
He watches over me
He loves, cares and protects me.

He has great expectations
And I am bound to do right by Him
To honor Him
To let his Light shine through mine.

He fuels my soul with His graces
He sends His angels to my rescue
Without Him I am just an empty vessel
I shall praise Him forever.

Thought on Tolerance.

"If you must; judge not Men by rumors, but by their repeated actions." – Joan AMBU

A Childhood Friendship

Growing up I was blessed to have a Father
Whose career took him all over the country.
While we never stayed long enough on a set location
My friendships only lasted for a little while.

In 1990 we finally settled down in Yaoundé
And not too long after moving into our home
A family moved across from us.
Smiles were shared
An unconditional bond was formed
Friendship was born right from the get-go
Between one of the kids and me.

Stéphane won my heart
And instantly became my best friend and confidant.
He was the kind and friendly guy from across our house
Who would bug and nag at every opportunity he had.
We spent every day talking, sharing and supporting
He was a huge source of compassion.

I cherish and hold those memories close to my heart
Those were joyful times
When life was so simple
Those were some of the best days of my life.

Though we last saw each other 15 years ago
I never stopped searching for him and asking around.
No one had the time nor the will to track him down
Including those I spoke to, who knew his whereabouts.

It made me wonder
If perhaps only fate could reunite us once again
As it was the case 21 years ago?
I couldn't help but wonder.

This morning I was blessed to reconnect with him
I jumped with joy as my heart leapt
With excitement and gratitude.
Today I feel warm and joyful inside
Just as I remember feeling as a child:
Free of worries and content
As I reconnected with my Childhood friend
As I look forward to new beginnings.

Remember —

As we observe, learn and become aware of our surroundings; we connect and advertently share bonds free of prejudice at such a tender age. Those are the individuals we tend to remember for the rest of our lives.

Nurture your childhood friendships.

About the Author

Born in Cameroon on September 9, 1980, Joan Ambu studied at Collège François-Xavier Vogt and College de la Retraite in Yaoundé, Cameroon. She enrolled in the University of Yaoundé I in 1999, but did not finish the academic year.

She flew to the United States the same year, where she studied first in Arkansas Henderson State University, then transferred to DeVry University in California for her Bachelors and Keller Graduate School of Management for her Masters.

Joan Ambu is part of a family of five children, the eldest, died in 1998. Her father, William Ambu is a retired Colonel of the Gendarmerie Nationale Cameroon. Her mother, Alice Ambu, studied in San Jose, California and has served in several courts in Cameroon.

Joan has always had a fondness for words and discovered her passion for writing at a very young age.
She uses writing to heal, to comfort others and to communicate with the outside World.
Her works are inspired by her feelings, relationships and especially the loss of her older sister in 1998.

Married and mother of two children, Joan now lives in California, where she exercises the art of writing.

By the same Author

La Rose Morose
Recueil de Poèmes (2011)

ISBN-13: 978-0-9836996-0-6
ISBN: 0-9836996-0-7

Printed in the United States of America by CreateSpace

Amour Extrémal
Recueil de Poèmes (2011)

ISBN-13: 978-0-9836996-1-3
ISBN: 0-9836996-1-5
Printed in the United States of America by CreateSpace

Nombre Impair (Hommage à Ma Sœur)
Recueil de Poèmes (2012)

ISBN-13: 978-0-9836996-2-0
ISBN: 0-9836996-2-3

Printed in the United States of America by CreateSpace

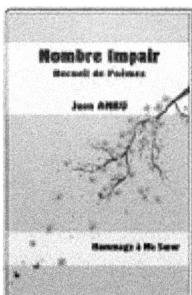

www.ingramcontent.com/pod-product-compliance
Lightning Source LLC
Chambersburg PA
CBHW060439090426
42733CB00011B/2331